CUSTOM-FIT
HUSBAND
READY-MADE
WIFE

Library of Congress Control Number: 2016936793

ISBN: 978-1-63308-225-0 (hardback)
        978-1-63308-226-7 (paperback)
        978-1-63308-227-4 (ebook)

Interior and Cover Design by R'tor John D. Maghuyop

CHALFANT ECKERT
PUBLISHING

1028 S Bishop Avenue, Dept. 178
Rolla, MO 65401

Printed in United States of America

CUSTOM-FIT
HUSBAND
READY-MADE
WIFE

A Woman's Guide to Molding Her Mate

LaQuenta Clarke

CHALFANT ECKERT

PUBLISHING

TABLE OF CONTENTS

ACKNOWLEDGMENTS

Thank you C.M., C.W., and J.C.

for your encouragement and feedback. It was instrumental in

pushing this project forward. I appreciate you.

PREFACE

———— ∞∞∞ ————

Can a husband be sculpted to meet his wife's needs, attend to her desires, and make her happiness his primary purpose in life? Yes, absolutely. If you are the woman who owns his heart, your husband can be trained. This guide is designed to show you just how to do so. What it cannot do is tell you if you have married or found the right partner. That is a decision you have made, hopefully in good faith.

Custom-fit Husband / Ready-made Wife: A Woman's Guide to Molding Her Mate will provide you with steps crafted to aid you and your spouse with fostering a joyful marriage. It awards you, the wife, with the secrets to remain firmly in control. Behind every strong man is a strong woman, guiding him in just the way she wishes him to go.

Here's how.

INTRODUCTION

My temples were moist with the sweat drizzling from my recently designed updo. I wondered if this form-fitting dress would hide my protruding stomach, thick with nerves, gas, and water weight, as I prayed my impending period would stay away just one more night. Two mothers stood with me in a dark, cramped, single-stall bathroom, and we all looked at the final product in the oval mirror slantingly hung above the sink. I wondered, would anything change as I turned the key from girlfriend to wife?

Let's face it. I had been in a relationship with this man for almost two years. There should be no surprises at this point, right? However, my mind still wandered to thoughts of relationships we both watched fall by the wayside in such a short period. Why didn't those relationships last? What would make my marriage different? Statements like, "She's going to change once you get her home," or "Don't let her change you," echoed from the man club. On the other side I hear, "Men are too needy, don't bother," or "He's going to make you sacrifice your needs for his," chanted from the bridesmaid's corner. Should I follow my career dreams first and get married later?

That was when my mother, about thirty years deep in marriage, shared with me the secret. She looked at me, turned my direction from the sink and with her water-filled eyes, she stated: "Baby, I know you're excited, and you feel as if you've gotten the best one. But Momma's got to tell you the truth. I had to learn this for myself. You can find a good man, but a husband does not come ready-made. They have to be custom-fit. Marriage is a lifestyle change. You cannot be married only in the bedroom. That gets old, fast. You will have to be married in all of your rooms." Then, after a moment of silence, I was given the secret that set my marriage on the path to success. "You have to train your husband."

As one might imagine, this is not a task easily accomplished. I didn't have a guide, nor did my mother provide the step-by-step process. However, she did state: "Your husband will be a direct result of you." This requires repeating, slowly—your husband will be a direct result of you.

WHAT IS A TRAINED HUSBAND?

Trained husbands will fit multiple definitions based upon the women they reflect. However, common traits will be found in every man who has been successfully molded.

Your husband will own his responsibility as the man of his house. Functioning as the man of the house means more than having the final word, and it doesn't require making the most money. It does require that he sacrificially put the needs of his wife and household first. A man, who is the true head of his household, does not rest until he knows the basic needs of his home are met. It also means he willingly places his desires secondary to his family's wants and needs. Your husband finds peace in knowing you are safe, satisfied, and happy.

Your husband will love you completely and respect your independence. A husband's true love is felt and not questioned. The ways in which he loves you will be remarkable to your relationship and known by you. He will not require you to become subservient for him to feel accomplished. Instead, he will support you fully, respecting your right to explore your full potential.

Your husband will share the responsibilities of your home. When your husband is properly trained, you will not feel you have to carry the full burdens of your home. He will be a partner in items important to both of you. This could be the after school pick up line or weeknight dinners. The most important aspect is he makes an effort to ensure your burdens are not too heavy to bear.

Your husband will communicate openly and value your opinion. Your spouse will take the lead in sharing with you in your partnership. He will make it plain that your thoughts matter, and he will not keep things from you.

Finally, your husband will live to please you! My marriage has now been the envy of elders, the separator of friends, and the spotlight of fulfillment. What does this mean? Have you ever lost the companionship of a friend because she could not cease emotions of jealousy when in the presence of you and your spouse? Adversely, have you been told there is a different feeling one receives just by being with you and your partner? One knows that he or she is in the presence of true and welcoming love.

TRUE AND WELCOMING LOVE

True and welcoming love is a love that is genuine, secure, and not threatened. Have you experienced strangers whispering in your ear, "I can see how much that man loves you"? I have.

For a while, I felt guilty. I sensed our joy should not make others unhappy. I knew, subconsciously, there was nothing I could do to curb their jealousy. Besides, like everyone else, I deserved to be happy. If they were not happy in their own relationships, that was something I could not control. I also know life experiences that are exponentially good or bad should be used as tools to help someone else. Therefore, I was provided this unattainable joy to aid others in finding the same.

I share these steps with you based on observations of failure, stories of success, knowledge from my studies, and wisdom from my elders. Most importantly, I have unlocked the secret by charting my own story.

I love my husband, and I know he loves me, every second of every day, without question. I do not doubt or wonder where my husband is or whom he may be with. My children have a great father, and I have a confident spouse, lustful boyfriend, and intriguing partner.

Put forth the effort and you can too. It is not too late. Failure is neglecting to start.

CHAPTER ONE

Gain His Respect

STEP ONE

Know Who You Are and What You Want

Take this step most seriously. If you are not able to master the concept of this chapter, you will not be able to train your husband. Part of love is the desire to please or make one happy. You must first desire to please yourself. Know what you want out of life, and define what it takes for you to be fulfilled. What brings you joy? Who are you, and what do you want during this life? Visualize your end-game.

Do not expect your husband to complete you. This is a magical movie myth. Yes, you do become one in marriage. You may feel more complete. However, do not bring your husband jagged, worn out pieces of your personal puzzle. He may grow weary of trying to put the pieces together.

If you do not know what fits, how will your spouse? Women sometimes approach a relationship with the thought that a man will bring to them the very piece of themselves they are missing. If you are searching for completeness or something that will make you feel whole, it can only be found by searching within yourself.

Do the following statements reflect your beliefs?

I believe I can be happy by myself.

It is important to live honoring my individual beliefs.

The activities I choose and the places I spend my time bring me a feeling of satisfaction or joy.

I know what I want to accomplish tomorrow, next month, and next year, and I take full responsibility to see my objectives are met.

There may be pieces of myself I need to work on, but they do not define me. They are works in progress that I will address accordingly.

I take responsibility for my own life, no matter what unexpected occurrences I may encounter. Ultimately, I must define what brings me peace.

If you successfully embrace the aforementioned statements, chances are you will feel whole with or without a partner. If you struggled with some of the concepts, take steps to answer your own questions. Seek counsel, redefine your agenda, speak to your spiritual leader, or embrace the support of family and friends.

Many paths can lead to the completion of your personal puzzle. However, you are the only person who can determine where the pieces fit. Only you can determine who you are.

Use Your Past as Fuel to Build Strength, But Don't Bring Issues With You

We all go through something. Some feel as if the burdens they bear are too much for others to comprehend. This may be true. It would be a mistake to bring these issues with you. Deal with them before you say I do. Your relationship comes with its own challenges. There is no need to bring the old ones with you. Do bring the lessons you learned as strength for future endeavors.

One might ask, how do you resolve an issue of a memory, a pain, or an undeniable occurrence in your past that has unintentionally aided in shaping you?

Let's start with the word *issue*. An issue can be defined as something that is in question. It can also be defined as a matter or occurrence in dispute. Therefore, resolving the issue you are experiencing means you will have to define it. Know fully what the matter is and how it has affected you. Acknowledge your issue; then begin to transform it. Transformation will involve four steps:

- Define and Acknowledge: The first step, as described earlier, is to define the issue. Know fully what your issue is and acknowledge how it has affected you.
- Forgive: Determine what is required to forgive those involved. If it was a self-inflicted wound, you will have to forgive yourself. If it was something done to you, forgive the other person.
- Decipher the Lesson: Decide what lesson was learned from the experience. Some good can come from every bad situation. Yes, every bad situation can somehow bring about good. This can be a lesson learned, wisdom gained, relationships formed, or a number of character building items. Once you have set your heart to forgive, let your mind decide upon the lesson.
- Implement a Plan: Implement a plan to turn the lesson into a positive character trait, fuel for the future. You do not want to be hurt again nor do you want to harm your partner by somehow projecting negative feelings or expectations from the past upon him. Therefore, a plan is required.

At this point in the process, you have defined your issue, acknowledged how it has shaped you, decided to forgive, and defined your lessons learned. You have everything you need to formulate a plan to implement in your future. When this is done, the issue will be resolved or left behind. The examples below will illustrate the four steps of issue to fuel resolution.

Let's consider the example of physical abuse from a partner in a past relationship. When a woman is physically abused it leaves scars that cannot be forgotten. There is angst, anger, confusion, and a host of other emotions that will need to be acknowledged. This will be the first hurdle. Find the counsel needed to define and acknowledge how the occurrence has affected you.

Next, you must forgive. Yes, forgive the person who has harmed you. Forgiveness, as described many times, is more for you than it is for the other person. Carrying symptoms of hate with you is unhealthy. Besides, in order for someone to inflict harm on another person, there must be a pain within him or her. Pity may be a more accurate emotion. Forgiveness is taking power back for you. It means you will no longer dwell on what happened, intentionally cause yourself to hate or hold a grudge, and you will do your very best to move forward. Wish the offender well.

What lesson did you learn? I imagine one lesson is abusive relationships are unhealthy and should be avoided. The resulting scars are physical as well as emotional.

Now, determine how this negative past experience can be transformed into positive fuel. This is a particular issue one should not wish to bring into a new relationship. The following are just a few items that come to mind, there may be many. Take steps that allow you to recognize traits of abusive behavior. In the future you will spot these traits early. Learn self-defense or martial arts. This will give you a sense of comfort and confidence. It also builds strong character. Avoid surrounding yourself with those who belittle, insult, or make you feel negatively about yourself. Instead, welcome uplifting relationships.

Consider this example. A woman experienced molestation by a trusted male role model as a child. The experience left holes that needed to be addressed before she could move beyond the wounds. Some were apparent, while others she was not aware of until later in life. This occurrence was transformed into fuel in the following ways:

First, she acknowledged she felt afraid and alone following the occurrence. She did not recognize what had occurred, and she did not know who she could trust with her story. She felt it was partially her fault, and it should be kept a secret. Shame, fear, and lack of trust were the emotions intertwined in her actions. These emotions contributed to very guarded and withdrawn personality traits. As a married adult with children, the woman eventually acknowledged she felt a great deal of unwarranted apprehension and fear when faced with leaving her child with anyone, including close family members. One should always be safe, thoughtful, and calculated when leaving a child in the care of any individual. However, her apprehension was to the point of anxiety.

She eventually recognized the root of her actions and acknowledged their source. This allowed her to move forward. The woman forgave herself and the person who molested her. The molestation was not her fault. She shared her story with close family, and also received counsel from a professional.

An important lesson learned was to make it clear to her children the difference between good and bad touch. Feelings of trust and openness are required in a parent-child relationship, and it is the parent's responsibility to build the foundations of this relationship early.

Part of her plan or fuel going forward was to use the past to equip her own children to be knowledgeable, confident, and comfortable with asking for help in questionable situations. They were taught before kindergarten that no one, not Mommy, Daddy, brother, sister, cousin, or friend was to touch them in a way that made them feel uncomfortable. Ongoing conversations occurred regarding sex and negative life experiences throughout their childhood. This included teachings of how to recognize potentially bad situations. They were given a sense of comfort that they could talk to her no matter what or whom the subject entailed.

This issue or negative occurrences has now been transformed to a past experience that has made her and her family stronger.

As stated earlier, do not bring old issues into your new relationships. These relationships will have their own challenges. Instead, concentrate on bringing your best self, fully equipped with fuel from your past life experiences.

Walk in Confidence, and Have Faith in Your Beliefs and Goals

What brings you joy in the moment? When you know which items release you or bring you peace, plot a path to achieve them. Confidence comes from knowing the very things that bring you joy. This includes both large and small things. What outfits make you smile? What hobby exhilarates you? When do you feel most accomplished?

Don't be swayed by society's norms and neglect your own personal beliefs or desires. You cannot walk confidently when you are trying to fit into someone else's mold. Be yourself. Plot a path to achieve that which makes you happy, and you will begin to walk in confidence. Set goals and stick to them. This will propel you forward instead of holding you back.

Feelings of accomplishment and self-worth rub off on those around you as positive energy. Likewise, feelings of not being fulfilled and loss can be life draining. Not following your personal path can reflect upon your husband as fault, blame, or resentment.

There will undoubtedly be detours, bends, and bumps on your path. Adjust. Do not give in.

One of my goals was to earn a graduate degree. This task took more than a decade to complete. It survived marriage, two kids, four jobs, several relocations, and three schools. However, I wouldn't have changed one thing. I enjoyed life and grew through the struggle in the interim.

Growing up in a single-wide trailer in the midst of poverty, I felt my dream couldn't reach beyond my front door. In my neighborhood, one rarely pictured oneself in jobs that did not involve clocking in and out or wearing a uniform. My eyes were set upon a different path. I wanted to dress in a suit for work and brush elbows with "the boss." Well, "the boss" would soon take direction from me.

Life will happen on the way to your goals. No matter how you plot your path, you are going to have to navigate though many detours. Enjoy it, learn from it, but do not see it as a hindrance or a failure. Reevaluate, adjust, and move on.

KNOW WHAT YOU EXPECT
IN A HUSBAND

No, a good husband does not come ready-made. Your expectations of how you expect to be treated, what you will not tolerate, and the definition of feeling loved are things you define, before you continue in a marriage. Disrespectful or demeaning behavior overlooked once, will happen twice. If allowed twice, it will not only continue, it will worsen. Try to make the first the last.

My husband was fifteen minutes late for our first date. After ten minutes, I changed from my date attire into my night clothes, and I began to settle in for a night of TV and coffee. When my date arrived, I let him know—very loudly and angrily—we would not be going to the movie. I stated if he really wanted to be with me, he would have been fifteen minutes early! At the time, I had no phone. My date explained to me he did not have my address, and he had to find a mutual friend to guide him to my home—who, by the way, was with him to confirm. My response? You had twenty hours to figure it out!

Did the date still occur? Absolutely, this was a strong and determined man. My strength only ignited his intrigue and competitive spirit. However, he knew in no uncertain terms, I would not allow myself to be mistreated. This applied to the current date or any date that would follow.

Surprisingly, I learned very early in life to demand respect from a man. If you start a relationship as a doormat, you are almost assuredly going to be walked on frequently. Do not hesitate to acknowledge when your feelings have been hurt or when you feel wrongly treated. Throughout your marriage, pay attention to your RADAR. R -Recognize you have been offended or committed an offense, A- Acknowledge it is a concern, and it matters, D-Discuss the situation with your husband, A- Apologize or Accept an apology, and R-Resolve the issue together.

R - Recognize unacceptable behavior
A - Acknowledge the offense
D - Discuss how the offense has affected each of you
A - Apologize or accept an apology
R - Resolve the issue together

Failure to take the actions to recognize your personal RADAR can and will result in grudges—either by you or against you. Consider the case study below.

Case Study: Low Tolerance for Grudges

I grew up in a household of abuse, isolation, and secrets. Love abounded in the midst of these items; however, it was like living in a game of double-dutch jump rope. You never wanted to get tangled in the ropes, but you enjoyed being in the game! One item I witnessed was my family's ability to hold a grudge.

As the middle girl in a family of four, I developed some of the stereotypical traits of introversion and social longing. I took others' feelings personally, and I never wanted to feel as if I was shut out. I needed a place to feel safe and accepted unconditionally. Early in my adulthood, this was also what I sought in a relationship.

Fast forward to the night of the rap concert, the second official date I would have with my future husband. I planned my outfit all day, and I knew I was fabulous. This was the problem. I arrived with my girlfriend at the Marine Corps barracks to meet my then boyfriend, and he had a welcome crew waiting. Let's just say I was on display for this proud peacock.

One hour passed, and we were running dangerously close to being late for the concert. I interrupted the male banter (for the umpteenth time) to nudge my boyfriend towards leaving. However, he was more interested in asking me to wait while he called yet another friend to have a brief discussion. Well, the same way I arrived was the way I decided to leave. I politely, perhaps abruptly, told my boyfriend, "I'll see you at the concert."

That evening, when we arrived at my home, he would not say one word to me. In fact, he managed not to say a word for two days while remaining firmly in my presence as much as possible. This not only frustrated me, it also amazed me that one person could manage to hold a grudge so strong. I had seen a glimpse of this grudge holding side before. Apparently, my mate was famous for his innate ability to silently, yet maliciously let his anger be known. I did not realize at the time that I too could be a recipient of this special treatment.

It was clear he desired to be with me, and I with him. Therefore, I made my conditions known. I told him, in no indefinite terms, he would never hold a grudge against me and remain with me. We would resolve all issues the day they occur. To do so is simple respect.

Did the conversation go smoothly? No! However, it was worth it. Weeks later, he revealed that my boldness to challenge him and demand his respect was one reason he fell for me. He knew that day, he wouldn't be able to run over me and do whatever he pleased. I wouldn't allow it.

Never go to bed with unresolved issues. My husband and I have remained true to this promise ever since. It is a cornerstone of our marriage. When we wake, the day always begins anew because we did not take anger to bed.

You may not be consciously aware of all the items you desire in your marriage. It is important to know that most of these items have already been defined. They develop over your entire lifetime, starting in childhood. If it makes you feel less than, belittled, or neglected, this is something you should not tolerate from your partner. To gain your husband's respect, you must know who you are and what you expect from a husband.

Confidence is sexy, independence is desirable, and self-actualization is inspiring. Master these traits and you will win your husband's respect. You must have three things to train your husband successfully: his love, his respect, and his hunger.

CHAPTER TWO

———— ⊶⊷ ————

Be the Drug

STEP TWO

Help Him Resist the Temptation to Stray

In order for your husband to resist the street temptations, he must feel he has something better at home. Yes, I know, you've heard this before. Have you been told how to be the drug? Two factors will keep your husband coming home. Becoming his drug is the first. The second we will discuss in the next chapter.

The desire for another hit of you must be the whisper in your husband's ear that compels him to come back for more. How do you become his drug? Follow the advice below to have your husband craving you long term, not just for the spring-filled moments of your first years.

TIPS TO BECOMING THE DRUG

Get high off of your own supply. Be the object of your own affection. As mentioned in step one, you must love yourself first. Do what makes you feel at peace and complete. If I am unable to escape to the gym, indulge in my weekly thrift store scavenger hunt, and maintain my biweekly manicure, I feel less than my best. What is your "all about me" indulgence? Remember, it could be as simple as an afternoon stroll you use to relax, stay fit, and reflect.

Feel good about yourself. Confidence with a touch of arrogance is inviting. A woman is best in life, in social gatherings, and in bed when she feels she is presenting herself at her best. If you do not feel good about yourself, you are unable to share yourself fully with anyone else.

Do not neglect your personal appearance. Do not primp more for your job or your social group than you do for your husband on a lazy day or before you go to bed at night. This does not mean you put on full makeup and heels on your day off. It does require you know how to adorn yourself so you feel desirable. This usually equates to you looking desirable to your spouse. My favorite short nighty, a pair of bootie bedroom shoes and my hair in a bun is more than enough for an evening in. It feels much more desirable than a flannel house dress that used to sometimes call my name. However, if the flannel does it for you, go with it! Find what makes you feel sexy and stick to it! The important thing is that you feel your best in his presence. This brings about the confidence mentioned earlier.

BUILD UP, DO NOT TEAR DOWN

Feed his ego. Men thrive on ego and sex. You must feed both. As women, we tend to forget that men require just as much attention as we do. They constantly question if their status as a man meets the world's, and especially your, definition of success and appeal. Compliments, considerate actions, and a well-placed "I am proud of you" are not just reserved for women. Your husband needs a consistent flow of these items from you, or he may crave to receive them elsewhere. Make sure your husband knows you desire him and he is appreciated.

Avoid continuously highlighting what your husband does wrong or his areas of imperfection. A constant stream of negative comments blend together as nagging. More often than not, this will make coming home dreaded. Therefore, training will be far from your reach.

This does not imply you should not address the issues that cause you concern. It only indicates your method to discuss these concerns should not involve belittling or constantly insulting your spouse. The crucial element is in implementing the timing, tone, and delivery technique.

- Timing – Consider the time you broach the subject. What is the mood of the room? Are there other people around? The best time to have an uncomfortable conversation is when both parties are rested, alone, and open to listen. In other words, the moment one or both of you get home from work may not be the appropriate time.

- Tone – Anger begets anger. A loud voice or an accusatory tone will prompt defensive behavior. When you choose to speak with your partner regarding items that irritate or anger you, pause to make note of your tone. It should be conversational at best.
- Delivery – How you say it is just as important as what you say. Pay attention to your body language. Folded arms, raised eyebrows, and pointing fingers will not receive the listening ear you seek.

Know the desired end result. Have the remedy in mind before confronting an issue. Contemplate the damage that was or will be caused. Be able to explain to your partner why addressing the concern is important. For example, your husband piles shoes and work tools at the front door.

Incorrect: (With loud voice and wagging finger)

I'm tired of stepping over your shoes and tools in the doorway! Either you pick them up or I'm going to toss them out the door!

Correct: (Conversational voice, relaxed)

Sweetheart, I left a basket by the door. Please use it to store your shoes and tools. When you leave them in front of the door, it becomes very easy for someone to trip over them. Thank you.

ADJUST TO ACCOMMODATE GROWTH AND CREATE A PLEASANT ENVIRONMENT

As you mature in your relationship, change will occur. To keep your spouse's interest, you must adjust your actions to accommodate these changes. Just because ponytails, miniskirts, and tight t-shirts turned him on at eighteen does not mean he will still be attracted to these things at thirty-five. Dance clubs may no longer be the event of choice on the weekends. Maybe a game of golf or a hiking trip is a thought and a whisper away. Pay attention to the items that pique your husband's interest. Incorporate some of these changes to keep your spouse intrigued and thirsty. Drastic changes are not necessary. There is a lot to be said about subtle tweaks to behavior.

Nest. At the end of each day, is your home a comfortable place to relax? Think about it. When you are tired, relaxing at a spa would sound great, wouldn't it? Adversely, if you are worn and tired, do you really want to step over toys and dirty clothes, wonder what you will eat, and hope there is a spot in the house were solace can be found? Part of accommodating for growth is also recognizing the changing needs of your home environment.

Ensure your home is a desired destination at the day's end. There are a number of ways to do so, and it does not have to be totally dependent upon you (See Chapter Five – Define Roles Early and Often). Your goal should be to draw your spouse into the spa of his own home. Like many other circumstances, if he cannot find peace at home, he will seek it elsewhere.

Do not underestimate the power in this step. It is just as important as the others in becoming your husband's drug. The thought of a comfortable home can be the greatest enticement. (See Chapter Five Case Study: Wife Now the Other Woman, for an example of nesting gone wrong.)

When you become your husband's drug he will do whatever it takes to have you. Like an addict, he will want to protect you and keep you safe. Most importantly, he will desire to be in your presence whenever he can.

Case Study: Cat Daddy

Have you ever considered sending a man a teddy bear and flowers? What about sending them to a six-foot-four inch, two hundred sixty-five pound, hardcore Marine?

When my husband and I began dating, that is exactly what I did. After our first few dates, I wanted to send him something to let him know how special he made me feel. As naive as I was at the time, no one ever told me it was not customary for a woman to send a man flowers. Besides, at the time, this is what I did for a living. What better way to flex my muscles than to pour my heart into an arrangement created just for him? I picked the most masculine stuffed brown cat that I could find, tethered it to my newly-created floral masterpiece, and had it delivered to his office at the Parris Island Marine Corps Recruit Depot.

As one might expect, upon arrival his fellow Marines had a field day teasing him about what could have possibly happened the night before to make me send him flowers. Others had a few threatening words to say about his masculinity, very few (remember, this was no small Marine). Then, one of his friends stated, "You are going to marry that girl." To this he replied, "I know."

Every man may not appreciate flowers, but all men enjoy being appreciated. Let him know he is special.

CHAPTER THREE

⚬⚬⚬

Make Love All Day

STEP THREE

Make Him Look Forward to Coming Home

Unfortunately, some of us think back to the times when we were dating with both joy and regret or loss. We remember the fluttery-butterfly feelings we experienced at the sight of our partner because we held recent memories of the gestures of love expressed. We reflect upon items such as an unexpected love note left behind or grunt of lust tossed in our direction as we walked out the door dressed to impress. How many different words did he use to tell you he loved you? When did this excitement dwindle? Why?

When a relationship begins, we tend to make love all day. No, this does not mean you physically have sex all day. While the sound of this is quite intriguing, it's not practical. What I am referring to is a bit easier to do. Give your partner what you want, and you may receive it in return. Think about it. There are some things each of you did consistently when you began dating that made you want more of the other's attention. It could have been something as simple as a pet name coupled with a seductive look reserved only for you. Whatever these items were, they made you feel special and loved throughout the day.

Unlike the first two steps, there are no typical norms to help you craft your methodology for making love to your husband throughout the day. Your relationship is just as unique as the two of you. As stated earlier, if this area of your relationship is not where you want it to be, give him what you want. For example, if you want breakfast in bed, cook it for your husband. Do this without expectations, just out of love.

Eventually, you may find that desire to reciprocate your actions of affection may outweigh your need for attention.

Try to incorporate the unexpected. Keep things interesting. My rule of thumb is, whenever my husband is on my mind, I attempt to let him know. If I am feeling like I need attention, I give it. If things start to be routine, I switch them up a bit. I no longer have to initiate these things as much. My husband now has the same type of approach.

QUICK TIPS TO ADD MORE SPICE TO YOUR MARRIAGE

The following tips may seem simple to some, audacious to others, or a mixture of both. These tips are meant to provide spontaneity and variety options. All may not work for you and your marriage. Some are elementary, but they must be said. The overall objective is to keep each other smiling. Use them as inspiration to create your own techniques within your comfort zone.

Enjoy each other!

Use touch to your advantage. In some ways, men are indeed like dogs. They like a little rub, brush, or caress anywhere … on the head, behind the ears, scratch the tummy, rub his back. They all work. It only takes a moment, and it can be done at any time. I do mean any time. It is expected during lovemaking. However, a gentle touch of love is not necessarily expected while driving or as you walk by him standing in the kitchen. Use your hands to express what's in your heart. If it is lust, let the direction of your hands express this. If it is adoration, convey that. Has he been working out? Maybe using your fingertips to gently run down his biceps or his abs will state, "I see you, and I like where this is going." You want your husband to know you are feeling him (pun intended). In turn, his attention is directed towards you.

Don't use sex as a weapon. Do use sex as a surprise, an afternoon snack, or a much needed getaway. The more you do it, the more you want it! Likewise, the greater the time in between sessions, the least likely you are to initiate spontaneously. Remember, your genitalia are muscles. They need to be exercised to remain vital for years to come. To keep your sex life healthy, the most important thing you can do is make love as often as you can. In other words, find the time, and make the place.

We often hear of couples stating they have lost their desire for sex. Although some reasons for this occurrence are medical, my belief is most times this experience is self-inflicted. If you find yourself wondering why you and your spouse do not enjoy sex as often as you once did, first consider what you have done to cultivate your love life. Also, consider how many times you've refused or decided against having sex.

No one likes rejection, even within a marriage. Do not assume your partner knows you want him, and do not use sex as way to express discontent. If you do, you may also find the pistol pointed in your direction since you will also experience the pain.

Keep him blushing. Give his prize organ a name, and speak of it often. This allows you to speak openly yet discretely in public places or in mixed company. Let's call it John… "Honey, will you please tell John I am sorry I missed him yesterday. I will definitely see him tonight." This is your husband, let your imagination take over. If you want to make your husband blush, try this, and be creative!

Drop him a line. You're at your desk at work. An hour long meeting has just ended, and your head is pounding from the nonsense that was once again discussed at length. You hear a familiar tweet from your phone letting you know you have a message. It reads… "Your sexiness is on my mind, as usual. I can't work under these conditions!" Would you smile? So would your husband.

Make him laugh. Learn how to make you husband laugh. What sparks his funny bone? Be willing to laugh at yourself. Humor is an excellent way to temporarily alleviate the pain brought by the burdens of life. Look for opportunities to turn mundane afternoons or serious situations into humorous tasks. Then, when you reflect upon them, instead of grimacing, you may smile.

Be silly. It's okay.

Find time to connect. It becomes increasing difficult as the years go on to make time for each other in a marriage. This is especially true when kids and careers are put into the mix. Don't use any reason as an excuse not to find time to spend with your spouse on a frequent basis. This applies no matter how valid the excuse may be.

Remember, time together doesn't necessarily mean a nice restaurant or the movies. It could be a walk, thirty minutes on the couch between bottle feedings, or a trip to the grocery store before picking the kids up from soccer practice. The important thing is for the two of you take time to appreciate each other's company. Keep watch for the times when your paths cross, uninterrupted.

An overlooked, yet imperative, time to connect is when you both meet at the end of the work or school day. What do you do in the first moments, the first few minutes you see each other? Do you give each other a peck on the lips, or do you take the time to give a passion felt kiss? Have you ever pulled him into the room, closed the door, and really said: "Hello, I missed you"?

How was your day? When you and your spouse have this conversation, is it sincere or routine? Does he have your complete attention? Do you appreciate what the day's challenges were for your partner? Being your spouse's drug requires you being a calming presence at day's end. He can be the same for you.

Remember maintenance. I love my car … when it is clean. I enjoy riding in a comfortable clean car. Therefore, I do all I can to keep it that way. Upkeep is important, especially when it comes to the things you care about and the places where you spend your time. Not only do you want them to last, you want to keep them in the best condition possible. This also applies within a relationship. Most likely, you were first attracted to your husband's appearance. This was a primary reason you wanted to be close or intimate with him. It still is. Therefore, if you like your husband in blue, buy him blue shirts. Tell him how handsome he is in the blue shirt since it compliments his skin tone. Sell it and he will adopt it. Whatever works!

Do you want your husband to be conscious of his weight? Pay particular attention to the foods you both bring into the house, the restaurants you choose to patronize, and the amount of exercise you work into your daily schedule.

Create opportunities to develop desired maintenance habits.

Words matter. The words you use in your everyday conversations matter. Words convey more than the obvious message within sentences. The manner in which you use your words can convey emotions such as respect, love, and appreciation or the lack thereof.

When we meet strangers or interact with friends, we are very conscious of the words we use. In these moments, we know the words and the nonverbal cues behind these words will convey a message—intentional or unintentional. Be purposely conscious with your partner as well. Control your message.

My husband very rarely refers to me or calls me by my given name. When he is in the midst of a conversation he says, "I told my Baby," or "My Baby said," or "I was talking with my Baby." When he calls me, it is usually preceded with Babe or another affectionate name I choose not to share. My name is not usually a fall back for him. In fact, when he uses it, I am usually the impetus. I can be overly conscious of our public adoration.

The point is, his words always let me know where I stand. They are definitive and possessive. I am his and he loves me. This drug belongs to him. Why would one question love when it is constantly wrapped in the sentences you use with one another?

Be the drug ... Doing these items will focus your husband's hunger towards you. You will be his drug. Like any other intoxicating item, he will be under the influence of you. As the old saying goes, "He is putty in your hands." Mold with care.

CHAPTER FOUR

———— ∞ ————

Define Roles Early and Often

STEP FOUR

Encourage Your Husband to Carry His Weight

Man is a universal term. It can be used to describe a man and woman in general terms. Woman is very distinctive. It is singular referring to a specific sexual being. Therefore, as you approach the time in your relationship when you begin to define roles, know that all roles are not interchangeable. In addition, the male was destined to hold a stronger role. Let him!

This statement is not meant to negate the fact that men and women become partners in a marriage. It doesn't imply that you cannot be a strong woman. In fact, you must. It does indicate you cannot hold both roles. Marriage requires a delegation of tasks. Training your husband requires you trusting him to be the man of your heart and an authority in your home. It also mandates you support him in doing so. This is where the training takes place.

HOW TO DEFINE YOUR ROLES

Don't let society dictate what is right for your marriage. You and your partner are unique in your wants and needs. The design of your virtual marital contract should keep your stimuli for joy in mind. Remember, happiness is the ability to live life and find joy daily in the moments, acts, statements, and beauty of our reality. The desire for marriage is knowing your spouse will increase this joy exponentially. You will be dependent upon each other. Marriage is a codependent relationship. There is no need to do it by yourself.

Don't ask and don't tell. Shut the world out. Do not let any outside individual dictate what the roles should resemble in your marriage. Who does what, when, and how is going to constantly change as life takes you on a ride. Your marriage is as unique as you and your husband. Soliciting exorbitant amounts of unprofessional advice, complaining to friends and requesting their opinions, or modeling your relationship after someone else's may backfire. Therefore, images or roles that you may see from other couples in society or on television are of no use when you come to the negotiating table. Plot your own path.

Treat the amount you choose to share of your relationship with a long-handled spoon. Keep each other's confidences. Remember, while you are venting to a family member, you are also shaping their opinion of your spouse. This may be perceived negatively by your husband, and he will be much less likely to conform to your ideals. In fact, you will likely receive the opposite response.

When you and your husband decide to move on, your friends and family members may still be holding a grudge. They were not a part of the fight nor the make-up. Venting only provides them with your version of the story, your angry opinion of your spouse, and the one-sided image which begins to take shape.

Know the limits. As you begin to learn your partner, you will realize there are certain character traits that can and cannot be changed. Knowing these traits is important in a negotiation. You must first accept your husband for the core, unedited man you fell in love with. He will not magically turn into the perfect husband the moment he he says, "I do." Behavior is habit-formed. Habits are norms or learned traits that are casually developed taking into account outside influences. You are now his greatest outside influence. Be patient.

Listen and be observant. Actively listen to what your spouse needs, desires, and wants. Defining roles requires wisdom and understanding. Fulfilling your needs becomes more important when your husband feels that his needs are equally important. Therefore listen attentively during conversations.

Study the woman in his life whom he admires most. What are her traits that he adores? What does he consider a good woman? You probably share similar traits. After all, he did choose you. Enhance or maintain these traits. Keep in mind, this woman may or may not be his mother.

Communicate. You cannot get what you want if you do not let it be known. Your husband is not a mind reader. If you feel overwhelmed, say so. If you need help, ask for it. The key word here is *ask*. Discuss options with your spouse. Try not to go into a discussion or negotiation with your solution in mind. Ideas are great. However, do not assume you are the single best source of answers for change. This will hinder your ability to listen.

Don't castrate your spouse. As strong women, we tend to have a "can do" attitude. Along with this attitude may come impatience. Once your husband takes on a role, begins a task, or asserts authority in an area, let him. The more of the traditional, ingrained male roles you take on—such as protecting, providing, and sheltering—the more you lower your husband's expectation or sense of urgency to do these things. Adversely, you raise his expectation that you will take care of them. You have entrapped yourself in this instance. When you no longer want to function wearing your two-sided cap, it will be most difficult to reverse the damage that has been done, since the expectation has gone. Share the load.

Ultimately, a man must feel wanted, depended upon, secure in his manhood, and in charge. No, this does not mean in charge of all things or in charge of you! (If this is your concern, it may also be a control issue that needs attention.) Marriage is an admission that you want the companionship, and more importantly, the partnership of a man. Therefore, he has a role to play. If you prefer to "do it all yourself" it may be a good idea to examine why you got married.

I have a take-charge personality. I can confidently say I am an overachiever and an in-charge person at work. At home I am not very different. One thing that brings me peace is the fact I do not have to be in charge! My husband married me knowing I did not need him. I could take care of myself. He stayed because I chose to depend on him. I rest in the comfort of knowing I do not have to do it all. My husband is capable and willing to care for me in any way he can.

Don't allow what you cannot afford to continue. Fear is a crippling emotion and comes in many forms. In a marriage, it sometimes causes one to avoid conversations that must be held to avoid hard feelings, anger, or discontent. Sometimes, roles are left undefined because the thought of the conversation makes us uncomfortable. Would you rather be uncomfortable for a few minutes or miserable for years?

For example, many of us women feel overwhelmed at the tasks we tend to take on in a marriage. Oftentimes, we do this on our own accord. Regardless of the reason, if you need help, ask for it. Laundry, chauffeuring, cooking, mowing the lawn, and bill paying all need to be completed. There is no reason the responsibility cannot be shared. I despise doing laundry, but I do not mind folding clothes. My husband washes, and I fold. Get the picture?

Remember RADAR. It works here too! R -Recognize you have taken on too much (you hurt yourself), A- Acknowledge it is a problem, and it matters, D-Discuss the situation with your husband, A- Accept his help, and R-Resolve the issue together.

R - Recognize unacceptable behavior
A - Acknowledge you have a concern and it matters
D - Discuss your feelings
A - Apologize and accept help
R - Resolve the issue together

Recognize - Acknowledge - Discuss - Apologize - Resolve

Consider this example. Your spouse is out late with friends and he returns home at five o'clock in the morning. He did not call nor did he have any excuse for being out so late other than, "I passed out." He has never stayed out this late before. Would you ignore this situation under the 'boys will be boys' excuse? Would the fear of the impending argument keep you from stating what you really feel? When you ponder how to respond, ask yourself this question: Can I tolerate this long term? Why or why not?

You and your husband are both adults. However, you are no longer single adults. You have to consider the impact your actions have on your partner each time you make them. A role you both share is to hold each other accountable for each other's actions. Do not allow what you cannot afford to continue. Embrace RADAR and the Timing, Tone, and Delivery technique (from Chapter Two). They will be needed throughout your marriage.

Case Study: Wife Now the Other Woman

Under what circumstances would you consider the wife the other woman? Had this question been posed to me in the past, I would not have been able to explain a scenario that would satisfy this inquiry. One would think something dramatic or life changing must have happened to cause a husband to act more committed to his mistress than his wife, right?

I cannot answer that question, but I can describe one scenario that provided me with a bird's-eye view. An acquaintance of mine complained on multiple occasions that her husband would not come home after work. On the weekends, he would rather fish all day than spend time in the house. When he wasn't fishing, he always had an alternate excuse.

Under normal circumstances, I would ponder the reasons why.

His wife was a young, beautiful, strong, and intelligent woman. Together they had a beautiful daughter. At the time, this was a stay-at-home mom completing her college degree. This was a woman who worked hard daily, and tried her best to make sure her child did not want for anything. Ideal wife, right?

This was my impression, until I got to know her a little better. My first step into her home was extremely calculated and careful because there was no place to put my feet! Let's just say hoarders had a lot in common with this wife. Besides the obvious lack of cleaning, her personal maintenance while at home was not a priority. Additionally, I later gained insight that her husband was the primary cook and homemaker.

This husband eventually told his wife he had been having an affair with a woman from work. He would often come to work and confide in this woman regarding his disdain with his home life. He worked long hours daily, and not only did he come into an unclean home, most times he could not rest until he prepared the meal. The first time he ventured to her home, she had lured him with the promise of a hot meal. It is probably important to mention, he had been teased with her cooking. She brought him hot lunches to work ever since she heard of his dilemma.

He eventually started going home to the other woman nightly. The nightly visits turned to sleepovers. Subsequently, he and his wife separated. He made a new home with the mistress.

My husband had the occasion to speak with this disgruntled spouse during the time of the affair. He stated his reason for straying was exhaustion. He wanted a clean home and a hot meal on a consistent basis. He was tired of wearing both hats. He believed he made his request known, but it fell on deaf ears.

The moral of this story is that role definition is important, because the jobs must be done. Had that husband used RADAR and taken the time to overcome his fear of the conversation, then maybe things would have turned out differently.

Be the drug.

CHAPTER FIVE

Share Your Spiritual Beliefs

STEP FIVE

Ensure Your Paths Are Aligned

When you entered into your marriage, it had a specific meaning to both of you. Marriage, in its barest essence, was created from the religious belief that a man and woman should come together as one to create a family. What that family consists of is completely dependent upon the couple. The same can be said for the marriage.

The belief that cannot be changed is your definition of marriage at the time you made your union. The reason you said "I do" had a very clear meaning to you. It was the ideal that you wanted to carry forth for the rest of your life. Did you and your husband agree? If your ideals of marriage differ, then your definition of what a marriage should and should not be probably differ as well.

Everyone has a spiritual belief. If you are an atheist, that is a belief as well. Stemming from these ideals are questions that will undoubtedly be pondered throughout your marriage, especially as it pertains to goals, roles, and child rearing. These questions become more intense within an interfaith marriage or within a marriage when one partner may be active in their faith while the other is more passive.

I will not attempt to guide you through the complexities of this can of worms. However, keeping in line with the objective of the guide, there are actions that can be taken to influence your husband to align your spiritual paths.

DEFINING YOUR BELIEFS

Have the discussion. Speak with your spouse about his spiritual beliefs. Know what is important to each of you as it relates to the intended path for your family. The earlier you ask, "What are your religious and spiritual beliefs?" the better off you will be as you grow to know each other.

In chapter four we discussed knowing your limits. There are certain character traits that are in essence, an ingrained part of your partner's personality at the time you both met. When you continue in your relationship, you must accept these traits as a part of his core. They will be most difficult to change. Therefore, knowing your differences early is essential.

Set the example. Practice what you preach. The grass looks greener on the other side of the fence. Be the greener grass. It is much easier to live following your own beliefs than to hide them for various reasons. If you do this, there will be one definite outcome. Your husband will know your faith is important to you. Hopefully, he also sees it makes you happy. He may desire to be involved (if he isn't already).

Do not push.

Case Study: If You Go, He Will Follow

> In my early days, I was a bit of an antagonist. I would throw questions at my husband (boyfriend at the time) just to see how he reacted. When I questioned him about his religious beliefs, it didn't dawn on me how much I was depending on hearing my ideal response, "I believe in God, and I am a Christian." My intent was to taunt him by calling him a heathen if he stated otherwise.

In my heart, I was Christian. In my actions, at the time, I was far from it. The one thing I seemed to know subconsciously as the words, "What do you believe?" slowly left my lips was that I could not stay in a relationship with a man who did not believe in God. I had been grounded as a child in this faith and its teachings. It was a part of me, even if I needed to find my way back to it.

His response to me was that he believed in God, but he didn't believe in organized religion. I could work with that!

As we both matured, I began studying the Bible and attending church. It troubled me that my husband seemed to have no interest in going. The more I asked, the greater he resisted. I even tried to guilt him into it. That was profoundly unsuccessful.

I confided in my mother. This was an extremely rare occurrence as it relates to my marriage. She told me these words, "Just keep going. As you learn, bring a bit of your lesson to him in casual discussions. Do not ask him to go again, and do not push. This man adores you; he is protective of your time and attention. Eventually, he will be curious, and will want to see for himself where you are going and why it interests you so. Keep going, and he will follow."

Just as my mother predicted, he did get up one morning and go with me. It wasn't instantaneous, but it happened. His initial reason for going was to please me, and align our paths firmly. He desired to make me happy. His decision to keep going had nothing do to with me.

Your husband's spiritual beliefs are just as strong as yours. If you find your paths are not aligned, do not try to force your beliefs upon him. The likely outcome is that it will drive you further apart. This is why this type of discussion is very important in the beginning of a relationship. My best advice is to keep the conversation active, and remember your RADAR when the discussion becomes difficult.

CHAPTER SIX

The Real Secret

I f you haven't figured it out by now, the true secret to training your husband is controlling your own actions. Your spouse is a reflection of you primarily because of his response to your nurturing, encouragement, and love. These are the positive actions you should embellish upon your spouse. Likewise, traits you would least like to see in your spouse will heighten due to the conflict, animosity, unresolved issues, secrets, undefined roles, and other draining traits that could have developed over time.

Yes, it goes both ways. You are also a reflection of your husband. There is one distinct difference. Just as the woman cannot be the man, the man cannot be the woman. Women have a unique way to contribute. As women, we were born with the innate ability to nurture. This is a gift.

Nurturing, according to dictionary.com definitions, is to support and encourage. It is also defined as the action of training and developing. This is a wife's strength. She can support and encourage her spouse in a way that leads to the training and development of a contented, loved, strong, and confident man who leads his household.

With this gift comes a great deal of power and responsibility for your contributions to the direction of your marriage. Nurturing is not mothering. Your husband needs a wife, not a mother. Throughout the book we discussed ways of nurturing and supporting your spouse. The more you love and nurture him, the more apt he is to respond to you in any way he feels it pleases you. It's that simple, but it is hard work.

Stop thinking of your husband as just your best friend or partner. Think of your husband as you would yourself. After all, he is a part of you. You became one in marriage. When you grasp this concept, you realize a new comfort. As you give, you receive.

In order for a woman to have true power in a marriage partnership, she must relinquish it. You cannot do it all yourself. When you invite a man to share your life, you have to make space for him to contribute meaningfully, in ways that give him pride, authority, and independence. Failure to do so results in a power struggle.

Your marriage is a work in progress. It will not be perfect from the start. It will probably never be perfect. Nothing is. As you define roles throughout your union, you can adjust by using your RADAR, communicating with one another, showing love continuously and creatively, and growing together spiritually on your united path. With these steps, your marriage will develop into your place of love, respite, joy, and safety. In the words of my husband, your husband will breathe for you.

Below is a summary and self-assessment for the steps outlined in this book. Use this as a guide to determine where your strengths and weaknesses lie as you continue your journey of moving forward in your marriage.

Step One: Know Who You Are and What You Want

1. I am satisfied with who I am right now.
2. I am able to enter into relationships as fresh starts, without looking for past hurts in my new partner.
3. I believe happiness is found in moments, and it is my responsibility to know how to release those moments in my own life.
4. I set short- and long-term goals for myself with the intent of furthering my own self-worth.
5. I have my own definition of what I expect in a man; it includes how I wish to be treated.
6. I will not allow my partner to belittle or disrespect me, and I am not afraid to take action if it should occur.
7. I consider myself a confident woman whom expresses her independence freely.
8. I am successful in letting my wants and needs be known and respected by my partner.

Step Two: Be the Drug. Help Him Resist the Temptation to Stray

1. I love myself, and I find ways to spend time with myself on a regular basis.
2. I am happy with the way I look.
3. I know the parts of my body and personality that my partner finds most appealing, and I take the liberty to enhance these features.
4. I find ways to compliment my partner daily.
5. In the past twenty-four hours, I told my partner thank you and I love you at least once.
6. I am able to complete the next sentence. Last week, I told my partner I appreciated the way he…
7. My house is clean and comfortable.
8. I do not look for ways to verbally or physically assault my partner, even when I am irritated or angry.

Step Three: Make Love All Day. Make Him Look Forward to Coming Home

1. My partner and I find ways to spend time alone together that we both find enjoyable.
2. I enjoy sex with my partner regularly.
3. In the past twenty-four hours, I have expressed love to my partner in ways not associated with sex.
4. I make my partner laugh daily.
5. I am physically attracted to my spouse, and I express it often.
6. I know how to make my partner blush, and I intentionally do so whenever I can.

Step Four: Define Roles Early and Often. Encourage Your Partner to Carry His Weight

1. I do not depend heavily on my family and friends to help me shape my marriage.

2. My partner and I speak often about our wants/needs and likes/dislikes regarding the running of our home.
3. My partner and I share most of the weight when it comes to errands and household chores.
4. When my partner begins a task and fails to complete it to my satisfaction, I do not take over and complete it myself. If needed, we discuss the issue.
5. When I feel overwhelmed, I ask for help.
6. I am willing to compromise and make changes I feel will benefit my marriage.
7. I do not avoid difficult conversations. Instead, I pause, reflect, and carefully consider my statement.

Step Five: Share Your Spiritual Beliefs. Ensure Your Paths Are Aligned

1. I know my spouse's spiritual beliefs.
2. My partner and I share the same ideals of marriage.

Interpreting the Results

This assessment was designed to highlight areas of your relationship that need to be strengthened. If you answered *no* in any category more than once, this may be an area needing attention.

Each step focuses on a particular section of the book. Re-read the section should you have questions.

Most importantly, this survey is for you. Answer honestly for best results.

APPENDIX

—⊶⊷⊷⊶—

My husband and I are Christians. Therefore, our aligned life path has been shaped with certain ideals regarding our future together. Most of these were subconsciously molded. When you are raised in a certain faith, some steps are just "built in" from memory and child rearing. For those of you who share this belief or are simply curious, I have provided some of the teachings that shaped the writing of this book. I thank God for every sentence. May it bless those who read it.

FOUNDATIONS:

KJV - The Bible, King James Version

NIV - The Bible, New International Version

Book Concept: Union of marriage, wife's innate ability to nurture (help/support).

> *And the LORD God said, It is not good that the man should be*
> *alone; I will make him an help meet for him.*
> Genesis 2:18 KJV

Book Concept: Husband lives sacrificially to please wife.

> *Husbands, love your wives, even as Christ also loved the church,*
> *and gave himself for it;*
> Ephesians 5:25 KJV

Book Concept: Let your husband take care of you. Acknowledge his authority as head of household.

Wives, submit yourselves unto your own husbands, as unto the Lord.
Ephesians 5:22 KJV

Book Concept: Make love often. Don't use sex as a weapon. Be the drug.

The husband should fulfill his marital duty to his wife, and likewise the wife to her husband. The wife's body does not belong to her alone but also to her husband. In the same way, the husband's body does not belong to him alone but also to his wife. Do not deprive each other except by mutual consent and for a time, so that you may devote yourselves to prayer. Then come together again so that Satan will not tempt you because of your lack of self-control.
1 Corinthians 7:3-5 NIV

Book Concept: Build up, don't tear down. RADAR.

Better to live in a desert than with a quarrelsome and ill-tempered wife.
Proverbs 21:19 NIV

Book Concept: Strong, self-assured, capable woman who knows who she is and what she wants. Woman who has the respect, love, and admiration of her husband. Nurturing wife.

The Virtuous Wife

Who can find a virtuous woman?
For her price is far above rubies.
The heart of her husband doth safely trust in her,
So that he shall have no need of spoil.
Proverbs 31:10–31 KJV (verses 10-11 shown)

ABOUT THE COUPLE

Eighteen years, two kids and counting. Karl and LaQuenta Clarke have been blissfully married for eighteen years. Their union has lasted over twenty years packed with numerous tests of faith, patience, and perseverance. The constants that keep their union cultivated is their shared spiritual beliefs, love unbounded, and mutual support for each other's individuality.

Karl and LaQuenta both feel called to motivate others to reach their full potential. Therefore, they founded QzUE Enterprise, LLC. This company's sole purpose is to use the written and spoken word to enlighten, inspire, and unlock genius in the people served. Part of this ministry is the passion to help couples strengthen their bonds.

QzUE Enterprise, LLC offers, among its multiple services, mentoring sessions and open discussions on the topic of marriage. We are always delighted to receive invitations to discuss this book.

Should you wish to hold a session for the group of your choice, please contact us at info@qzue.org or visit our website at www.qzue.org

Note from the Publisher

Are you a first time author?

Not sure how to proceed to get your book published?
Want to keep all your rights and all your royalties?
Want it to look as good as a Top 10 publisher?
Need help with editing, layout, cover design?
Want it out there selling in 90 days or less?

Visit our website for some exciting new options!